Christian Principles for Managing Money

James S. Poore, II

Foreword by Pastor Jeffrey A. Johnson, Sr.

Foreword

By Pastor Jeffrey A. Johnson, Sr.

Jesus spoke more about money and material resources than He did about any other topic—more than about prayer, more than about God's Kingdom, more than about fasting, more than about witnessing. Obviously, He wanted the Body of Christ to realize the importance of handling our material resources properly—and the ease with which we can be tempted to misuse them. Too many Christians allow physical, material, and monetary concerns to hinder their walk with God.

It is always refreshing to meet a Christian writer who truly realizes the value of keeping material things in perspective. James Poore is one such person and, in this book, he has given us a great resource for managing our material resources to please God, bless our families and communities, and advance the Kingdom. He takes a very practical approach toward using the Word of God to understand godly financial principles, and toward explaining how to apply these principles to our lives in the most productive ways.

As senior pastor of Eastern Star Church in Indianapolis, Indiana, I have for many years witnessed James teaching these principles through various conferences, workshops, seminars, revivals, and worship services, as well as through our JEWEL Bible Institute. Through his ministry, many individuals and families, and also our church as a whole, have become more competent in handling the material resources with which God has blessed us.

Now, James is sharing these same biblical principles with a larger audience through this book. His writing will make an enormous difference in the lives of all who adopt and adhere to these God-given insights. *Christian Principles for Managing Money* will be tremendously valuable to anyone who is serious about living life to please God and about reflecting a relationship with Him through His Son, Jesus Christ, in all areas of life.

I highly recommend this book to all Christians committed to financial integrity, who realize their accountability to God as good stewards.

Table of Contents

Acknowledgments

I thank God for giving me the opportunity to write this book. Our awesome Lord has once again done exceedingly and abundantly more than I expected. To God be the glory!

Special appreciation to Jeffrey A. Johnson, Senior Pastor of Eastern Star Church, and to his wife, Sharon, for the immeasurable impact of your ministry and friendship. I am very thankful for the opportunity to grow and serve under your leadership. You two are such an encouragement to Pamela and me.

I appreciate the encouragement and prayers of Pastor D. L. Page, Deacon Wright, and all the Eastern Star Church family. Each of you has been a blessing to me and my family, and we thank you for the roles you have played in my development and in helping to make this book a reality.

Thank you, Mommy and Daddy, for introducing me to Christ. The Christ-centered home in which you two raised me laid the critical foundation for my growth. I did not always agree with your rules but, as I have grown older, I realized you knew best. I have never gone without anything I needed, thanks to you two. Thank you also to my siblings and their families: Kelly and husband, Dell; Sherri; and

Tony, wife Dedee, and daughter Maya.

Pamela, you are the love of my life. I thank God every day for blessing me with you. You have been very patient and understanding as I have grown and served, and I appreciate your support. God surely recognizes how well you have aligned yourself with His role for a Christian wife. Trey, Bailee, and Kyndal—we both love all of you. The joy you have added to our marriage is priceless.

Proceeds

J ames and Pamela Poore will donate all proceeds from the
sale of this book to the JEWEL Christian Academy
(JCA) general operating fund. JCA, an elementary school, is
sponsored by Eastern Star Church, but is a separate entity
with its own 501(c) (3). The Academy is committed to
providing quality education based on biblical principles, so
that all children may be fully equipped to function in a
global society.

Eastern Star Church founded JEWEL Christian
Academy in 1995, when church leadership felt a calling
from God to help prepare the children of our community for
future success. Guiding principles are biblical application,
character development, and partnership with parents. JCA is
proud to serve children through our modern facility and
dedicated staff. For additional information or to make a
donation, contact JCA at:

JEWEL Christian Academy
5750 East 30th Street
Indianapolis, IN 46218
(317) 591-7200
Info@jewelchristianacademy.org

Introduction

Is your commitment to Christ the most important thing in your life? If so, that relationship should be reflected in all areas of your life—including how you manage money. The way you spend money is actually the best visible indicator of your innermost values. If I had copies of all the canceled checks and credit card statements you have accumulated over a lifetime, I could write your biography without ever meeting you personally—and it would probably be a better biography than the ones your family and friends could write. Your spending records are your true life story; you spend money based on what you value most. What *would* people say you value most, if your spending habits were exposed for all to see?

If you value your commitment to Christ and desire to handle money in a way that pleases Him, this is the book for you. Since the Word of God often addresses issues of money and money management, the Bible was my primary information source in writing this. I have also built up a practical foundation of personal experience, however, through years of working in the banking industry, and through teaching classes in Christian finance. This book furnishes a blueprint for effectively handling money and receiving all the Lord provides for you. Whether you are living in relative financial freedom or in severe financial bondage, whether you are rich or poor by society's standards, the information in this book will be a blessing to you—as long as you are serious about your commitment to Christ.

CHAPTER ONE

Your Attitude Is the Foundation

The journey toward aligning your spending habits with the will of God must begin by assessing your attitude toward money. Your attitude is important for at least three reasons.

Why Your Attitude Is Important

First, attitude is important because it forms the basis—the foundation—of every other decision you make. If you have the right attitude toward money and money management, you should be applying Scriptural considerations to all your financial decisions—building your house on the rock, so to speak. Having the wrong attitude about money is like building your house on sand—which will not withstand time or outside forces. (See Matthew 7:24-27.)

It is also vital to have the right attitude because we spend about 80 percent of our waking hours thinking about money. [1] When I first heard that figure, my initial thought was, "No way!" Instead of dismissing the idea, though, I spent the next few days auditing my thoughts—and I discovered the statistic was not that far off. Between working hours (thinking about how we are making money), balancing the budget, planning our spending and savings, and just plain worrying about and wishing for more money, financial matters consume most of the average person's waking hours. If you take time to audit your thoughts, you'll likely find far more of them directed toward money than you ever realized. If you have the wrong attitude, think how much time you are spending each day reinforcing it.

Finally, the proper attitude helps keep you rooted. In today's society, we are bombarded daily with marketing messages from dozens of companies, all trying to convince you to buy their products. In a single commercial break, you learn that you can't be a "real man" unless you drive a certain truck, that you'll play better basketball if you wear a particular brand of sneakers, and that your teeth will be far whiter if you use a specific brand of toothpaste. If you watch television for just one hour a night, read two magazines a month, and drive through a shopping district and down a billboard-lined highway twice each day on your way to and from work... just picture the number of marketing messages to which you are exposed every day, week, and month. You need the right attitude to maintain the proper mind-set and mentality toward all those worldly messages. The next time you see an advertisement, remember that you are already somebody important regardless of where you live, what you drive, or what you wear—because you belong to God.

By now, you're probably thinking, "Just what *is* the right attitude?" I believe the proper attitude has at least three main components.

Components of the Right Attitude
First, the right attitude recognizes God's ownership.

Psalm 24:1 reads, "The earth is the Lord's, and everything in it, the world, and all who live in it." The word "everything" is all-inclusive; it leaves out nothing. So all the things you thought you owned are included in the "everything" God owns.

To become a smarter money manager, the first thing you must do is acknowledge God's ownership, and consciously turn anything you were trying to keep for yourself over to the rightful Owner. When I first started studying Christian finances, I found an exercise that was very helpful in this regard. Each participant completed a Quitclaim Deed, similar to the one used in real estate transactions for quickly transferring ownership to another person. On the spiritual Quitclaim Deed, we signed over to God all the things we thought we owned.

There was a big empty space on the deed designed for us to individually list everything. I would have liked to take a short cut and just write the word "everything," but now I am glad I decided to complete the exercise the way it was supposed to be done. Had I not individually listed everything, I probably would have shortchanged myself and never realized the full impact of that exercise. Since then, I have included a similar exercise in each semester of the financial course I teach. (I remember one student who listed eighty-eight things!)

Why don't you try this exercise yourself, right now? Take out a clean piece of paper, and write "Quitclaim Deed to God" at the top. Individually list on that page everything you thought you owned (or acted as if you owned) but which you now are going to relinquish to God, the rightful Owner. (Completing this exercise may take some prayer.) Once you're finished, thank God for allowing you to manage His resources, and pray for forgiveness for claiming ownership of the items on the list. Tell God that you are giving them back to Him, and ask for direction on how to become an effective steward of His resources. Finally, post the list in a spot where you will see it regularly as a reminder, and where you can add to it as necessary.

Now that you have positioned yourself as a steward of God's resources, the next step is realizing that accountability accompanies responsibility. God has entrusted some of His resources to each of us. The amount He has entrusted to me is different from the amount He has entrusted to you. But one day, each of us will be held accountable for managing God's resources, however many or few we had to work with.

Remember the parable of the talents (Matthew 25:14-30)? A man, going on a journey, left some of his talents ("talent" meaning a sum of money in Jesus' time) with three different servants. One servant received five talents, another received two, and the third received one. When the master returned, he summoned those servants to give account of how they had managed his resources. Two, who had managed the money well, returned it with profit and were rewarded. But the third had done nothing with what was entrusted to him, and the master transferred those resources to someone more trustworthy.

You and I will someday be in the same situation as those servants. There will be a day of reckoning when we will be held accountable for how we have managed God's resources.

The third component of the proper attitude is dependence on the Lord. Proverbs 3:5-6 reads, "Trust in the Lord with all your heart and lean not on your own understanding; in all your ways acknowledge Him, and He will make your paths straight." Note that this Scripture passage tells us to acknowledge Him "in all your ways," not in all ways except our finances! So often, we are willing to trust in the Lord in every area *except* finances.

I remember a cartoon that a friend e-mailed to me. A man was standing in a pool, about to be baptized. As he was preparing to be submerged, he held his wallet in his hand straight out in front of him, so it would remain above water during the baptism. That picture illustrates too many Christians' mind-set about money.

Before I became serious about my commitment to Christ, my sense of identity was tied to material possessions

—such as my car, clothes, and cash—or to my career. I was never satisfied with what I had or who I was. I constantly wanted more: something newer or better, the latest and greatest. But I was aiming for a moving target.

Soon after receiving my undergraduate degree, I obtained a job earning exactly what I wanted to make. In addition to my desired salary, I received a company car and great benefits. But after two paychecks, I already wanted more than I was getting. Solomon was right: "Whoever loves money never has money enough; whoever loves wealth is never satisfied with his income. This too is meaningless" (Ecclesiastes 5:10). In other words, money and material goods do not give life meaning, let alone provide true happiness.

It was not until I realized my identity is in Christ that I stopped aggressively pursuing worldly possessions. I still like having nice cars, clothes, and cash, but I now realize that connection to Christ and the resulting sense of contentment are far more valuable than any possession. I now live by the advice of Matthew 6:33: "But seek first His kingdom and His righteousness, and all these things will be given to you as well."

How Is Your Attitude?

Now examine your attitude to determine whether or not it lines up with the three components: recognition of God's ownership, a sense of accountability, and dependence on the Lord. If you fall short in any of these areas, you should make an attitude adjustment.

The best example of unwillingness to make an attitude adjustment is the rich young ruler. According to Matthew 19:16-24, this man asked Jesus, "What must I do to inherit eternal life?" After a brief conversation, Jesus told him to sell all his possessions and follow Him. The rich young ruler turned his back on Jesus and walked away because he didn't want to relinquish his wealth. He relied on his wealth instead of on the Lord. Jesus then explained to His disciples how difficult it is for a rich man to enter the kingdom of God because the more you have, the easier it is to place more trust in your stuff than in the Savior.

In sharp contrast is Zacchaeus, a wealthy chief tax collector who lived in Jericho. (His story is recorded in Luke 19:1-10.) Everyone was excited and wanted to see Jesus when He entered Jericho, but Zacchaeus was too short to see over the heads of the crowd. So he ran ahead and climbed a sycamore tree to get a look at Jesus as He passed by. What no one expected was that Jesus would want to get a look at Zacchaeus, as well.

Upon reaching the sycamore tree, Jesus called Zacchaeus down and said He would be the tax collector's guest that day—a radical proposal in a society that hated tax collectors even more than ours does! But after sharing dinner with Jesus, Zacchaeus emerged a changed man, repenting of his sins, giving half his money to the poor, and repaying everyone he had cheated four times over. Jesus responded, "Today salvation is going to come to this house."

Whether you're rich or poor needn't determine your attitude. Some rich people, like Zacchaeus, trust in the Savior instead of in their wealth; and some people who are not at all wealthy trust in their "stuff" instead of in the Savior. Take a look at your attitude to make sure you have the right one!

CHAPTER TWO

Planning for a Successful Journey

＋￫￩＋

One semester after I taught my lesson on attitude, a student quoted a familiar saying, "The truth shall set you free." Meaning that, once you know the truth about money and have the right attitude toward it, you will be set free from whatever financial issue or bondage you are trying to overcome.

Actually, that is only part of the truth. Hopefully, by now, you are developing the right attitude toward money; however, you probably do not yet feel completely free. The true meaning of the saying is, *"Applying* the truth shall set you free." Knowing the truth will do you little good until you start applying it.

This chapter is designed to help you begin applying the truths you learned in "Your Attitude Is the Foundation." You'll become a smarter money manager by following five principles.

1. Pray before making purchases.
Take time to say a prayer before you spend any of God's

money. Many of us pray when it comes time to buy a big-ticket item, but we really should be in the habit of praying before *any* purchase. If you believe God is the owner of everything, and you are only a manager, then you are making a spiritual decision whenever you spend money. Why would you make a spiritual decision without first seeking God's guidance?

The next time you plan an expensive dinner out, pray for guidance before you leave home. The next time you feel like purchasing a new outfit even though your closet is already full of clothes, pray for guidance. The next time you find yourself standing in the lottery line, pray to the Lord for guidance—and *not* that He will tell you what numbers to play or what ticket to buy! Make a habit of asking, "God, is this how You want me to handle Your money?" I believe He will answer whenever you pray that prayer with the right attitude and spirit. Always praying before you spend money will make a big difference in your spending patterns.

2. Spend only cash.

For the purposes of this principle, checks and debit cards count as cash. The essential point is that you must make a commitment never to spend money you don't have. That way, you have to immediately reconcile all purchases with your available resources.

If you go to the mall with $50 in cash, buying a $25 item is spending half your available money. If you are going to spend half of what you have available, you'll make certain the purchase is something you really need. People who rely on credit cards do not consider their available resources as limited to $50; they consider their available resources to be their available credit-card balance. When they see that $25 item, they do not look at $25 versus their "real" available resources of $50. Instead, they think in terms of how long it will take them to pay back the credit card company in light of how much they make a week, a month, or a year—or worse, they figure they can afford anything that falls within their available credit-card balance, and don't even think about the necessity of paying it back.

When figuring in terms of future rather than present resources, $25 represents a much smaller percentage, which makes it easier to justify the purchase. Then the buyer compounds the problem by making more $25 purchases at additional stores. Credit-card addicts usually lose track of how much money they really spend each month, calculating the "affordability" of each purchase by the same amount they used for all previous purchases—however much they have added to their debts since.

If you currently use credit cards, try this exercise when your next statement arrives. Do not open the envelope right away. Instead, first write on the back of the envelope every place you used the card that past month, and the amount of each purchase. After you have listed every use of the card that you can remember, open the statement and see how much you forgot. You will see how easy it is to overspend when using credit cards.

You aren't safe even if you pay your full balance every month. Consumers who use their credit cards on this basis still spend at least 24 percent more than those who operate on a cash-only principle. [2] Whenever one of my students argues with the idea that credit cards mean increased spending, I challenge him or her to prove me wrong by doing without cards for a month and seeing what happens. Invariably, a month or so later, that student whispers in my ear after class, "You were right. I did spend less money when I used just cash."

Cut up those credit cards. That is the most-needed and least-performed type of plastic surgery in this country. I encourage you to save only one major credit card, to be used only in absolute emergencies. To make sure it is saved for emergencies, never keep the card where it is easily accessible. Instead, store it in the freezer: Half-fill an empty coffee can with water, freeze that, and then lay the credit card on top of the ice. Fill the rest of the can with water, and return it to the freezer for storage. The card is available if you need it, but the time it will take for the ice to thaw will give you ample time to thoroughly evaluate your intended use.

I do encourage all my students to have debit cards because I realize that carrying a great deal of cash raises safety and security issues. Using these cards is just like spending cash. Purchase amounts are immediately deducted from your checking account—generally on the day of the purchase—so it is important to keep good spending records. Remember that debit or "check" cards can be used, like credit cards, to make or confirm reservations. These days, many banks allow unlimited use of debit cards without additional fees.

3. Record your cash flow.

It is important to keep track of your cash flow, which means your income and outgo. Keeping track of your income is usually easier, but always keep your pay stubs in case you need to double-check them. Recording your outgo is tougher, but more important. In the next five chapters, I will examine five major outgo categories: Giving, Taxes, Savings, Debt, and Spending. I give target percentages in some of the categories, but not all, because everybody's situation is unique. The only constant from one household to the next is the need to put the Lord first and to demonstrate that principle in the way you handle money. God will help you balance whatever is left.

Track your outgo in the five main categories for at least a month, and then calculate what percentage of your income is being spent in each category. I suggest you track your expenses daily, total them weekly, and add the weekly figures together after four weeks. Determine your monthly percentage by dividing those totals into your monthly gross income. Once you have a clear picture of your current situation, make plans for how you will handle money the next month. After that, divide every paycheck and other income into the five main categories.

It is important that you follow the same sequence this book uses. The significance of my category order is that it puts God first.

I cannot stress enough the importance of tracking your spending during the next several months. Improving your stewardship begins with recognizing exactly where you are now. People frequently ask me how they can become better stewards—usually under the impression that I can answer that question while we are standing in the church parking lot. I always ask them, "What percent of your income goes into each of these five categories?" Usually, they have no immediate answer to that question. Then I ask them, "If you cannot tell me where you are, how can I tell you where you need to be?"

Remember, a map is a very useful tool, but only if you can identify where you are on the map. If you become lost while traveling to a particular destination, you would first have to identify your existing location before you could find the route to your desired destination. Likewise, committing to become a better steward is nearly impossible if you do not know how your funds currently are being spent. The more you learn about your spending habits, the better you will be able to make any necessary changes.

4. Commit to a daily intake of Scripture.

Develop a routine of studying Scripture each day. You will find that the more you read and study the Word, the easier it is to understand and follow God's calling to be a better steward. I find it best to study early in the morning, when there are no interruptions from family, friends, or employees. This also leaves me the entire day to meditate on the Scriptures. It is amazing how often the Bible passage I read early in the morning furnishes me with wisdom and strength to handle a situation I encounter later that very same day.

5. Select an accountability partner or partners.

You need a partner to accompany you on this journey. Therefore, you must find someone to whom you are willing to give an account of your actions and motives. Most of us do not like to be held fully accountable because we feel that this is restrictive, or that it may force us to leave our comfort zones. Real accountability, however, keeps us on the right path.

Accountability is not always comfortable, but it is necessary. When we are not accountable, we feel free to do whatever our desires dictate, which can lead us on dangerous and expensive paths. Those who make successful journeys usually have companions with them, and others praying for their success.

To illustrate: I recently made a commitment to become more physically fit. Thus far, I have been more successful with this attempt than with several others I have made in the past few years primarily because I now have accountability partners who work out with me. There are days when I do not feel like running and working out, but I do not want to be the weakest link, so I join the others on schedule. There are days on which we agree to work out on our own, on which it would be easy to avoid the exercise, except that I know I will have to answer to one of my partners before that day is out. In financial matters, too, you will experience a more successful journey with a partner. Even if no one is available to accompany you on the journey, you can still ask someone to hold you accountable. Your partner should regularly ask you five questions:

1. Are you praying before every purchase?
2. Are you spending only cash?
3. Are you recording all your spending?
4. Are you reading Scripture daily?
5. Have you been completely honest in your answers to each of the previous questions?

Ultimately, it is God Who holds us accountable. He sees all and knows all; nothing is hidden from Him. But finding a human accountability partner will help prepare you for the day when you have to account for how you managed God's resources.

CHAPTER THREE

The Principle of Giving

꘎━━꘎

The first portion of your paycheck should be set aside for the work of God. This is the first step in the journey toward smarter money management. Different levels of giving are mentioned in God's Word. This chapter will describe two of them.

The minimum acceptable giving level is the tithe, or 10 percent of your gross income. I know you may struggle with the word "gross"; many of my Christian finance students do. Every semester, at least one person asks, "Why figure the tithe from my gross income? Why not my net income?"

Well, the Bible does not mention "gross" or "net" incomes, but it does tell us to give God our best, our first fruits (e.g., Exodus 23:19a)—not the leftovers. If that isn't enough, consider these questions: Do you cite your gross or your net income when applying for a credit card? Did you acquire your house or apartment based on gross or net income? Is your car financed according to your gross or your net income? Well, if things you buy for yourself are important enough to be financed according to your gross income, why should you shortchange something far more important—your commitment to Christ—by giving in accordance with your net income?

Also, do you want to be blessed according to your gross income or net income? Luke 6:38 says, "Give, and it will be given to you. A good measure, pressed down, shaken together, and running over, will be poured into your lap. For with the measure you use, it will be measured to you." In other words, God will give to you by the same measure you use to give to Him.

Finally, remember the Law of Reciprocity: You will reap based on the amount you sow. Have you ever planted grass seeds to fill a bare spot in your yard? If you plant only a few seeds, only a few blades of grass will grow. If you cover the bare spot with seeds, the area will be filled with grass. As 2 Corinthians 9:6 says, "Whoever sows sparingly will also reap sparingly, and whoever sows generously will also reap generously."

Christians, on the whole, are failing miserably in the area of tithing despite all the promises in God's Word regarding the rewards of giving. Malachi 3:9 describes the whole nation of Israel as being under a curse because the Israelites were robbing God of His tithes and offerings. We call down a curse on our families if we refuse to give according to the plan designed by God.

The main reason I hear people give for not tithing is that they cannot afford it—which usually means they do not have enough money left for a full tithe after they fulfill all their other financial obligations. The question is, how are you prioritizing your obligations? When I ask people that question, I usually get a blank look and silence for an answer. I then tell them to step out on faith, and pay God first.

One of the rewards of giving is knowing that your needs will still be met. As Philippians 4:19 says: "And now my God shall supply all your needs according to His riches and glory." That promise is conditional, however, despite the many people who try to claim the victory of this verse with no obligations on their part. Remember, the Apostle Paul wrote the book of Philippians as a thank you letter to the Christians in Philippi, who had helped spread the gospel by aiding Paul in his earlier missionary journey. Thus, he was really telling the Philippians that God would meet all their needs because they helped fund the spreading of the gospel.

Thus, if you have given little or nothing to fund the work of the church because you spent all your money on your wants, you have no right to expect that God will supply your needs. But if you have willingly given your tithe to further God's work, be assured that God has whatever it takes to satisfy any need you have. Remember Psalm 24:1? His riches include *everything*.

Let's look at Malachi 3:10: "'Bring the whole tithe into the storehouse that there may be food in my house. Test me in this,' says the Lord Almighty, 'and see if I will not throw open the floodgates of heaven and pour out so much blessing that you will not have room enough for it.'" That is a guaranteed investment. God challenges us to test Him in the area of giving. Nowhere else in the Bible does He ask us to test Him.

God also tells us what He will do when we test Him: He will open the floodgates of heaven and pour out a blessing so big we will not have room to receive it. The King James Version says "windows" instead of "floodgates," and I rather like the former word because it is easy for modern suburbanites to relate to it. Imagine that a window is the only thing standing between you and your blessing. Although you cannot touch what is on the other side of a closed window, you can usually see it. Your blessings may be very close to you because windows are rarely thick, but windows still are effective barriers. Hence, if you can see clearly what God wants to do in your life but the blessing has not yet materialized, examine your tithing habits. Remember, the verse says God will open the windows *after* you tithe. That may be the only barrier to your realizing God's blessings.

Now let's return to the imagery of "floodgates." Such gates are designed to prevent floods by holding back large volumes of water. If the gates were opened, a flash flood would race through the land beyond. Remember that floods are sometimes good things, and that a flood of blessings nearly always is! Imagine countless blessings for your life, all blocked by floodgates like piled-up water. Now begin to consistently pay your tithe—and then stand back!

Whenever you give a tithe, you are acknowledging that God is in control of the material aspects of your life and that obeying His commands is your first priority. Whenever you give *more* than a tithe, the additional amount is called an offering. God deserves offerings: Hasn't He given *you* more than the minimum? My wife and I try to give offerings on a regular basis. The tithe is the minimum, but nowhere else in our life do we accept the minimum. The house where we live is no mansion, but it is much better than a one-room shack. The cars we drive and the clothes we wear are not always the very best money can buy, but they are better than the cheapest. Why should we return only the minimum—as little as we can get away with—to God?

If you are honest with yourself, you probably realize that there are few areas in your life in which you settle for the minimum. Don't do it with God—He is much more important than a car!

Imagine the impact your church could have in the community if every member gave only a tithe. Now imagine that everyone also gave a large offering. Take a look at Exodus 35:1-36:7. The people of Israel gave so much money toward the new tabernacle that Moses finally had to tell them to stop because there was too much money coming in! How many modern pastors wish they had that problem? Few of our congregations come close to giving as the

Israelites did—more often, our pastors must beg us for donations. We should be willing—and feel privileged to be in a position—to give.

The poor widow in Luke 21:1-4 demonstrates the ideal attitude toward giving. She gave two small copper coins, which were worth very little, while the wealthy were offering much greater sums of money. Jesus commented that the widow's gift was far more valuable to God than those of the wealthy because the woman gave all she had. People who claim that they do not give because their small amount of money would never make a difference should look at this passage. God is more concerned with your attitude than He is about the amount you give; remember, God already owns everything anyway. Your giving is a demonstration of your faith, and "without faith it is impossible to please God" (Hebrews 11:6).

Let me close this topic by mentioning two bumper stickers I have seen. The first one—which I have seen many times—says, "He who dies with the most toys wins." That is the way society looks at things. People consider life a game: The goal is accumulating as much stuff as we can and when we die, the game is over. I much prefer the other bumper sticker, which I have seen only once. It reads, "Don't let my car fool you; my treasure is in heaven."

Make sure that you, too, have treasure in heaven. Pray, and seek God's guidance regarding how He wants you to improve in the area of giving.

CHAPTER FOUR

The Principle of Income Taxes

O nce you have given your tithe and offering, the second portion of your check should be applied to your income taxes. This is important because so many things around us—things we take for granted—operate on our tax dollars. Have you ever considered who pays for the multi-billion dollar highway system on which you travel? Your tax dollars help make that possible. Do you know who pays the police officers and firefighters who serve and protect our community? We do, with our tax dollars. I do not believe in avoiding taxes; I value and appreciate the services that our tax dollars provide. Nor does the Bible consider paying our fair share a mere option. Paul writes in Romans 13:7, "If you owe taxes, pay taxes," and Jesus told us to give to Caesar (the government) what is Caesar's. Paying taxes is our Christian responsibility.

I realize that, if you have a salaried job, the government takes out money before you receive your paycheck. When income taxes were first instituted, the government did not take deductions from people's pay; it was everyone's responsibility to complete the tax forms at the year's end and then pay what was owed. Predictably, many Americans could not or did not pay their fair share, and the government often lacked the necessary funds to operate efficiently. No wonder the government gave up on trusting individuals, and made employers responsible for collecting and submitting employees' income taxes. Personally, I think this is the preferable system, for both citizens and governments. When money is systematically taken from each paycheck, we citizens are protected from huge tax liabilities at the end of the year, and the government functions more effectively with funds coming in on a regular basis. Planning and implementing operations always seems to be easier when the budget consists of regular small sums.

In any case, you do have some control over the amount of money that is deducted from your paycheck. When you are hired for a job, the human resources representative usually asks you to complete a great deal of paperwork. One of those forms is always a W-4, on which you record your marital status, tax exemptions, and number of tax deductions. Your employer uses that completed form to determine how much to withhold from each paycheck.

At the end of the year, your employer sends you a W-2 form, which records your earnings for the year and the amount of tax withholdings. After receiving your W-2, you fill out your tax forms and submit them to the government. If you have taxes due—if your employer did not withhold enough—you must pay the extra. If your employer withheld too much, the government refunds the overpayment to you.

Most people want an overpayment, because everyone likes to receive refunds. I, however, prefer to come out owing a little. This is because an overpayment is really an interest-free loan to the government—a loan of money you could have deposited into savings, where it would be collecting interest. (If you want to lend money without interest, I'll be glad to borrow some of it—and I won't even make you fill out numerous forms before I pay it back!) On the other hand, if you owe the government a substantial amount at the end of the year, it can charge you an underpayment penalty. Either way, you come out behind if your withholdings are too far removed from your debt.

If you receive a sizable tax refund, *or* if you owe a great deal of money, I encourage you to examine your W-4 form. If your tax refund is $1,600 (which is fairly typical), because there are twelve months in a year, adjusting your W-4 could increase your take-home pay by $100 a month and still leave you with a $400 refund. Talk to your tax preparer about adjusting your W-4, or, if you use tax software, take a look at the questions that appear at the end of most programs. One of those questions should be: "Do you want to print a new W-4 to submit to your employer?" Answer "yes," and the hard work is done for you. Simply print, sign, and turn in the form.

Your human resources department is another resource for information on updating your W-4. Tell the representative you've found out that huge tax refunds are a sign of poor money management, and that you want to adjust your withholdings.

Another option is using one of the many Web sites that walk you through the W-4. (If you want to identify one through a search engine, use "tax estimator" or "tax withholding" as the keywords.) You'll probably need a recent pay stub to refer to while completing your new W-4. Once you're finished, you can print out the new form and turn it in to your employer. Do the actual work at home, though; unless it's an official part of your job, you are stealing time from your employer if you do it at the office.

Yet another option is utilizing a worksheet that can help you determine the number of withholdings to claim. I recommend the booklet *How to Make Sure You Have the Right Tax Withheld*, which can be ordered at www.aspen-publishers.com.

After you adjust your W-4, check your next few paychecks to make sure the changes have had the right effect. If necessary, make additional adjustments.

To insert a little personal experience: The first time my wife and I adjusted our forms to reduce overpayment, we aimed for a difference of no more than $200 between withholdings and total debt. After making the initial changes, we went to a tax expert and explained our situation and goal. She reviewed our situation and gave us professional input—free of charge. I can't promise you will find such a generous expert, but I do recommend a professional analysis. And there's nothing wrong with comparing prices first.

If you do receive a refund, no matter what the amount, try to resist the temptation of the "anticipation loan" for which someone may offer you a guaranteed quick refund. If you have gone all year without the money, waiting a few more weeks won't hurt. Rapid refunds come with high service fees, and whatever fancy names your tax filer might have for these, they mean money out of your check.

There is one possible problem with adjusting your W-4—if you are accustomed to getting a big annual refund, you may be in the habit of living beyond your means all year and counting on the big refund to bail you out. Ask yourself honestly if you do this, and remember that you won't be able to continue once your annual refund is reduced. Living beyond your means is a good habit to get out of in any case, and if you implement the rest of the principles in this book, you shouldn't have that to worry about.

CHAPTER FIVE

The Principle of Saving

＋═╌═＋

A ny family may face a financial crisis at the most unexpected time. The causes of such crises are many, but we might divide them into "rainy periods" (additional expenses pouring into your life due to illness or some other unexpected emergency) and "dry periods" (drastic reductions in income due to sudden unemployment or reduced hours). Some people retain enough resources to financially survive these situations, though they may have to drastically cut back their standards of living. The best approach, however, is to be prepared for such an emergency by saving for it in advance. You must make it a priority to deposit a portion of every paycheck into savings after your giving and tax obligations have been fulfilled.

If you are not saving or consider it unnecessary, consult Proverbs 6:6-8: "Go to the ant, you sluggard; consider its ways and be wise! It has no commander, no overseer or ruler, yet it stores its provisions in summer and gathers its food at harvest." It may be embarrassing to think of receiving financial guidance from an insect. But if the Word of God uses the ant as an example, it must be good advice.

The ant referred to was likely the harvester ant. These

ants set up camp near grainfields during the harvest season, and then build "private storehouses," collecting grain from the fields one seed at a time. Through such diligent work, the ant saves up enough to survive through the winter. Note two things: First, the ant has enough instinct to know there will be a dry season. Second, the ant instinctively exercises initiative in saving supplies for that upcoming dry season.

Now, dry seasons come to human beings as well as to ants, even if not as regularly or predictably. Do you have enough initiative to be saving up for your future dry seasons? Anyone who doesn't should be embarrassed to have less foresight than an insect.

Moving from the natural world to human history, let's look at Joseph in Genesis 41. Joseph was a young Hebrew who was sold into slavery in Egypt and later imprisoned on false charges. He had a reputation for exceptional insight, however, and one day he was summoned from prison to interpret two of the Egyptian Pharaoh's dreams. When Joseph told Pharaoh that Egypt was about to experience seven years of abundance, followed by seven years of famine, Pharaoh was sufficiently impressed to give Joseph the highest position in government. Joseph then set about preparing Egypt for the famine by having the country store up grain—just like the Proverbs ant. Once the famine came, the Egyptians had more than enough supplies to carry them through. Other countries, which had saved nothing during the years of plenty, were forced to buy food from Egypt.

Many of us are like those other countries. We fail to save while times are good. Then, when emergencies arise, we are forced to borrow from family, friends, or financial institutions. It would be wiser to follow Joseph's example.

Next, let's take a look at the principles of saving.

Your savings account should be insured. The Federal Deposit Insurance Corporation (FDIC) insures bank deposits; the National Credit Union Administration (NCUA) insures credit union deposits. Having the principal (the amount you invest), as well as the interest, insured by a federally backed agency will make it doubly certain that the money will be there when you need it. Most reputable financial institutions automatically insure all savings and checking accounts, but because many banks also provide investment accounts and since the difference is not always obvious at a glance, do make certain you know what you actually have. If you put your money into an uninsured investment, and if that investment is at a low point when you need to withdraw money, the available funds may be much less than you anticipated.

Additionally, your savings account should be liquid, so you can get your hands on the funds whenever the institution is open. If the money is tied up in a time deposit product, you may not be able to touch it until you have established enough reserves, or you might have to pay a penalty to withdraw funds. (More on this topic shortly.) If you keep your money liquid, you can take out any amount whenever you need it.

The last feature of a good emergency savings vehicle is interest. Try to find an institution that pays interest on checking as well as savings accounts. Many people don't even know if they *are* earning interest on their accounts, let alone what rate. It's better to find out everything you can about what you are earning—and also how often the interest is compounding. (The more frequently it compounds, the better.) If you know little about the specifics of your account, ask the institution for details—including how you might change a no-interest account to an interest-earning one.

Also, make sure your account is earning the maximum available interest. I once went to a bank to close an account we did not feel was earning enough interest—and found out that all we needed to do was have the code in our account profile changed. Our interest level was immediately increased, and we didn't even have to order new checks. We had never been aware of the alternate account option with the higher interest rate.

I also remember a similar experience from the other side, when I was working as a bank officer. We were in the process of purchasing another bank and consolidating its accounts into ours. It was relatively easy to match most of the accounts being purchased with similar accounts at our bank. The other bank, though, had one savings account that paid a very low interest rate, and had numerous customers with money in that account.

The simplest approach would have been to roll the account holders from that account into our existing, similar savings account. However, doing so would cost our bank several thousand dollars in interest each month because our account paid a higher interest rate. Instead, we kept the other bank's account as it was and continued our old account at the same time. After the two banks were consolidated, customers with the old bank's savings account could easily have increased their interest by transferring their savings into our other account—but few did. It pays to keep informed, especially if your bank has recently gone through any ownership changes.

Financial institutions also introduce, from time to time, new savings options to attract new deposits. They may or may not inform their existing customers of the new options; in any case, they are under no obligation to do so. Take the initiative; don't rely on the bank to automatically keep you up to date.

Make sure you pray for guidance as you seek the appropriate financial institution and level of savings—too much can be as bad as too little. Don't be like the rich fool in Luke 12, who thought he was preparing for an easy life by hoarding everything he could but died before he had a chance to enjoy that easy life. All he thought about was having everything he could possibly need or want. In the end, his goods did nothing for him. Save some of your money; do not hoard it all.

A more common mistake, though, is putting off saving anything because we leave ourselves nothing to save. Saving is the last thing on most priority lists in this consumption-oriented society, where people live way above their means and spend everything they can. You may have to reduce your current level of spending before you can begin a serious savings program. Start by evaluating your spending habits to determine where you can cut back or eliminate purchases and convert the extra dollars into savings.

Direct deposit is an excellent aid to consistent saving. After you determine the amount you will put into savings each month, go to your employer and ask to have that portion of each paycheck automatically put into your bank; or, arrange with the bank to automatically transfer savings from your checking account. That way, you will handle the money less and reduce the temptation to spend it before you really need it.

And don't think you must acquire a large amount of money before you start saving. Remember the harvester ant? A tiny creature, it could carry only one seed at a time, but it did so time and time and time again until it had accumulated a sizable savings. Be just like that ant. Save a little money at a time, and it will grow.

The ideal amount to keep in savings is at least six months of living expenses. Once you accumulate that cash reserve, you can think about investments and other ways to increase your return. You might want to start with certificates of deposit (CDs), where you agree to leave the money in a product for a certain period of time in exchange for a somewhat higher interest rate than you would earn with a regular savings account. You might leave a month or two of expenses in the liquid savings account while purchasing multiple CDs with different maturity dates—putting, say, one month each of living expenses into three-, four-, five-, and six-month CDs. If you lose your job, you will have enough in your liquid savings to tide you over until the first CD matures. If you stagger, or "stair step," the CD maturity dates, you can time your access to their funds so as to avoid paying any penalties.

Some people argue that you should invest your money in a better-performing product, one that can potentially earn you much higher interest. *Potential* is the key word. The strategy I outlined guarantees a predictable, reliable source of funds. With an emergency cash reserve, you need that security; the objective is not getting rich, but being assured that the money is there if and when you need it. Building wealth through investments is another matter altogether, one for which you should consult a qualified financial adviser after your savings rise beyond sufficient emergency funds.

Remember also that there are other reasons for saving besides maintaining an emergency cash reserve. I recommend opening other accounts for such things as vacations, school clothes, major purchases, retirement, and holiday shopping—saving in advance for special events makes it easier to stick to a cash-only spending policy. If your financial institution offers a Christmas-club account (which is not as common as it used to be), take advantage of this effective tool for controlling holiday spending. Otherwise, open an account you designate for that purpose.

To set up a special-event account, first decide how much money you intend to spend. Divide that amount by the number of pay periods left until the money will be needed, and arrange to have the resulting amount withheld from each paycheck and deposited into the account. If you cannot do without the amount you come up with, you are planning to spend more than you can afford, and you will have to reduce either your cost of living during the interim or the amount you intend to use for the special event. In either case, make a firm commitment to spend no more on the event than the total balance in your account when the time comes.

A savings account is rarely built by accident or luck. Commitment and planning are essential. If you don't think you have any money to save, the following tips should help you plan your strategy:

- Always pray before you purchase.
- Buy based on your needs.
- Change your mind-set toward managing money.
- Delay all major purchases for at least forty-eight hours.
- Establish a savings goal for each paycheck.
- Focus on Christ during the Christmas season.
- Give God at least 10 percent.
- Have faith that you can save a little money from each check.
- Invest more time in reading Scripture.
- Just do it.
- Keep a list of items you want to purchase.
- Learn the value of compounding interest.
- Manage your money with a purpose.
- Never spend what you do not have.
- Open your mind.
- Plan to spend less than you budget.
- Quit spending based on your desires.
- Review your objectives monthly.
- Spend only cash.
- Train your children in good stewardship principles.
- Use direct deposit to establish your saving habits.
- Verbalize your success to others.
- Write out your savings goals.
- X-out your consumptive attitude.
- Yearn to save 10 percent of your income.
- Zip up your current spending habits.

Thanks to Tracy Boyd, Darryl and Jamya Fisher, Danielle Walker, and Angie Williams for their input concerning this list.

CHAPTER SIX

The Principle of Retiring Debt

＋≒≒＋

If you have any outstanding debt—from a high credit card balance to a mortgage delinquency—you are a typical American. Today's consumers are acquiring debt—recurring payments on depreciating assets—at increasingly younger ages. The average debt load per household continues to grow. Credit-card delinquencies, home-equity loans, and mortgage delinquencies are at record levels. (Regular house payments do not count as debt in the sense used here, because houses tend to appreciate in value.) All these are symptoms of today's tendency to live above one's means.

Every Christian should live as debt-free as possible. The Bible doesn't tell us never to assume any debt, but it does warn of the dangers. As Proverbs 22:7 says, "The rich ruleth over the poor, and the borrower is servant to the lender." In Solomon's day, that was the literal truth—people could be sold into slavery to repay their creditors. That situation may not exist today, but borrowing still can put you in the figurative slave's position—your creditor effectively controls the amount of money you can spend on other things, and can even take your property if you cannot pay your debt. Hence, once you've paid your obligations to God, the government, and your future needs, the next spending priority should be debt retirement.

First, let's look at why people acquire debt. My own first experience with debt was due to lack of knowledge. When I received my first credit-card solicitation, all I saw was the monthly payment of $20. I did not bother to determine the number of months I would be paying the $20. Nor did I understand how quickly the interest would compound. I had run the card up to the limit before I realized what had happened; in fact, I exceeded the limit and was introduced to the "over-limit penalty." Credit cards are not free money; they always cost *you* money.

To further explain the impact of credit-card interest: Suppose that you have accumulated $5,000 in credit-card debt at 20 percent interest. If you pay only the minimum monthly payments and incur no additional debt, how long do you think it will take to pay off what you owe? It will take you 535 monthly payments—more than forty-four years! The minimum payments for the first five months will be:

- $110.00 for month 1;
- $109.41 for month 2;
- $108.83 for month 3;
- $108.25 for month 4; and
- $107.67 for month 5

—reduced by only about 60 cents per month. But all that time, the interest continues to compound. Approximately $82—nearly 75 percent—of the first payment goes toward interest. It will take 473 payments before the greater percentage of the minimum payment is applied to the debt itself. By the time all 535 payments have been made, you will have paid a total of $14,607.30—almost three times the original debt—and the $5,000 debt will have cost you $19,607.30.

Thank God, I was able to retire my own debt in considerably less than forty-four years, but I still wasted a great deal of money on interest payments.

Another reason for going into debt is peer pressure. Unless rooted in the Word, we are likely to fall into the "keep up with the Joneses" trap. Peer pressure comes in many shapes, forms, and fashions: a neighbor driving a new car, a co-worker wearing a new outfit, a fellow church member's move to the "better" side of town. As the saying goes, "We buy things we do not need with money we do not have to impress people we do not like." That is peer pressure. If peer pressure is a problem for you (and it probably is an issue, to some degree, if you are in debt), remind yourself that your identity is in Christ.

Remind yourself also of the consequences of debt. The biggest and most subtle consequence, with which I have personal experience, is a reduction in your current standard of living. Every dollar you pay in interest toward a previous purchase reduces your current standard of living by the same amount. If my neighbor and I make the same salary— but I have debt and he or she does not—then his or her current standard of living will be much better than mine. When my neighbor earns $100, he or she has the full amount to spend on current needs, wants, and desires. But when *I* make $100, most of that money will be applied to debt payments.

Fortunately, there are ways to get out of debt.

The first step is to confessing your sins—and you *have* sinned, by breaking a biblical principle, if you have mishandled God's resources. Confessing your sin opens the door for His forgiving and cleansing light to purify your heart. 1 John 1:9 says, "If we confess our sins, He is faithful and just to forgive us our sins."

Next, correct the difficulty that drove you into debt. Pray that God will reveal to you the reason for your debt and will give you clarity about how to overcome the problem. Most people who are in debt got there through the wrong attitude toward money management. Usually, they did not realize that everything belongs to God and that they would be held accountable; and they tried living their lives on credit cards without comprehending the financial impact. If you implement the principles discussed in this book, I believe you will be able to correct all issues that led you into debt.

Then, commit yourself not to assume any additional debt, not even a zero-percent financing offer. Remember to spend only cash and, if you do not have enough cash to buy something, live without it. Zero-percent and free-financing offers sound good when advertised, but fewer than 20 percent of consumers are ultimately able to meet the requirements—monthly installment payments toward the balance within the set time period, with the entire balance paid off on schedule—for the zero percent. The others pay retroactive finance charges, which instantly take effect in the event of a missed or late payment.

Now, to get rid of your existing debt, you need a well-organized plan. List all your creditors on one page (more, if necessary). Record (in three columns) the debt balance, minimum monthly payment, and balance- computation method (which should be listed on the back of your statement) for each creditor. Arrange the debts by creditor from the highest balance to the lowest. Add up the columns to determine your total debt load and your minimum-monthly-payment total. Include every regular payment, large or small, except your mortgage.

Then, be sure you are paying every creditor *something* each month. If you absolutely cannot meet a minimum amount due, contact the creditor to negotiate an alternative payment arrangement. Explain your situation, emphasize your commitment to pay something each month, and suggest an amount. Few creditors will turn you down. They would much rather receive a reduced amount each month than nothing at all. If you doubt that, consider: If you lent someone money for which the repayment arrangement was $100 per month, and he or she could not pay the entire $100, wouldn't you rather receive whatever amount possible than have the borrower "disappear" because he or she was convinced you wanted all or nothing? All creditors feel the same way. Slow pay is better than no pay. Run toward your creditors when you cannot fulfill your exact repayment obligations; never run away from them. Besides, they will likely catch you eventually and, if you have given them cause to doubt your honesty—which is exactly what you have done if you pay them nothing and avoid taking their calls—there will be no room left for negotiation. If you've been watching your Caller ID, so you can avoid answering calls from creditors, cancel that service, and apply the money you used to spend on it to your debt load!

Finally, don't be content with minimum monthly payments. In addition to paying the monthly minimum (or whatever you have agreed to) on each bill, pay something extra toward the smallest balance every month. Once your smallest debt is paid in full, keep paying out that money— add it to the minimum monthly payment for the next smallest debt. Continue this "ladder approach" until all debt is paid off.

If you're tempted to shortcut this well-proven, debt-elimination process by consolidating your loans—don't even think about it before giving yourself at least six months to cultivate the spend-cash-only habit. The "consolidation loan" idea—combining all your debt into one loan in exchange for a lower monthly payment with a lower interest rate—is often merely a means of treating the symptom rather than the disease. That is, excessive debt is only a symptom of the indiscriminate credit habit; if you assume a consolidation loan without correcting that habit first, you will probably end up in a worse situation than before. A consolidation loan should never be used as an excuse to buy more on credit, and should not be used at all unless you fully understand how it works and can truly use it to save yourself money. When evaluating a consolidated-loan offer, read the terms in their entirety, including the fine print. If it still sounds good, reread the whole offer at least one day later; you will pick up on new things. If you're still interested after the second reading, *write down* the answers to the following questions:

- How long is the introductory rate effective?
- Is the introductory rate effective on balance transfers?
- Are there any other transfer fees?
- What will the interest rate be after the introductory rate expires?
- What is the annual fee?

Then, if you're still convinced you can save money on this consolidation, go ahead.

One last thing. Once you're out of debt, never get back in. Make spending only cash a lifetime habit!

CHAPTER SEVEN

The Principle of Spending

F inally, we have reached the point where you can spend some money on yourself. By meeting all your other obligations first and saving this for last, you avoid spending what you can't afford. Now you can finally satisfy your own needs, wants, and desires.

You still have to be mindful of your spending, though. Prioritizing your purchases is essential. Start by addressing genuine needs, such as food, shelter, transportation, and clothing.

Beware of letting needs turn into wants. For example, transportation is a need. A high-luxury car is generally a want. Buying the most expensive car your income will allow, regardless of other financial obligations, may be a foolish waste of money. The need for transportation can usually be fulfilled with a reasonably priced used car, which is two or three years old. Before buying anything, assess your true needs and available funds thoroughly, and then choose the most economical vehicle you can.

Remember, desires should be met by purchases made from surplus income, which is to be used only after all other financial obligations have been met.

Remember, also, that Colossians 3:17 ("And whatever you do, whether in word or deed, do it all in the name of the Lord Jesus, giving thanks to God the Father through Him") applies to spending money on ourselves. *Every* category in which we handle finances should reflect our commitment to Christ. Since housing and transportation are the two areas in which people struggle most with spending decisions, the balance of this chapter will focus on them.

Housing

Most of us grow up taking shelter (housing) for granted because it's always there. When the time comes to buy our own homes, our lack of experience usually shows in our purchasing more home than we need. Even renters frequently choose larger places than they need, hampering their ability to save up down payments toward future home ownership.

Because a house purchase represents a long-term commitment that can be very difficult to get out of, the most important question to ask before buying a home is, "How much house can we afford?" This is a personal decision that should be made only after much prayer and a thorough review of your financial situation. Many homebuyers allow themselves to be guided by others who lack full understanding of the buyers' financial aspirations, goals, and expectations.

The best way to find out how much house you can afford is by subtracting your monthly tithe and offering, income taxes, savings, and debts from your monthly income. Compare the resulting figure to your monthly needs, wants, and desires. Then make a realistic decision about how much you can spend on a monthly mortgage. Keep in mind that home ownership involves many expenses beyond mortgage payments.

It's a good idea to buy less than what you think you can afford. If you're a couple, purchase your house based on *one* income. Counting on both your incomes puts too much pressure on you and leaves no margin for error—or for future changes in work situations. When it comes to paying off the mortgage itself, take a strategic approach. Say that you have a $100,000 mortgage financed at a fixed rate of 7.5 percent for thirty years. The monthly mortgage payment, including principal and interest, will be $699.21. Once interest is figured in, it will cost you $251,751.60—more than 2.5 times the original loan amount—to pay off the house in thirty years. The extra $151,751.60 is all interest.

Now, consider that each payment has a principal component and an interest component. Of the first $699.21 payment, only $74.21—just over 10 percent—goes toward the principal, the other $625 being interest payment. Your loan balance is now $99,925.79.

After a year, you have paid out $8,390.52 ($699.21 x 12) toward the mortgage. Nearly 90 percent of that— $7,468.74—has been applied to the interest, and you have paid only $922 toward the principal. Moreover, the mortgage will be past its twentieth year before the loan is reduced sufficiently for the majority of the payments to be applied toward the principal; on your 254th payment (twenty-one years and two months' worth), $350.15 will be credited toward your principal balance, while $349.06 will be credited to the interest.

You can see that, as with credit cards, sticking to the minimum monthly payment—taking thirty years to pay off a thirty-year mortgage—works against you. Suppose, instead, that you pay $750 every month instead of just the $699.21 minimum. Ask your lender to use the extra money as prepaid principal. (Remember, if there's a second income in your household, you can put part of it toward the payments even if you didn't mention that income while discussing your qualifications for the loan.) If you continue this approach for the life of the mortgage, you will save

$36,036.62 in interest payments, and the house will cost you only $215,680.60 and be paid off in twenty-four years instead of thirty. That additional $50 each month will be worth it in the long run.

Now, suppose that in addition to paying $750 a month, you make an annual prepayment of $1,000 toward the principal. By the time the mortgage is paid off, you will have saved $64,933.94 in interest and will have your house for $186,783.28 and nineteen years of payments—less than two-thirds the required time!

Principal prepayment options may involve much smaller amounts than listed here. Any prepayment, at any time, will make a difference. Weigh the possibilities carefully. Also, when initially considering a mortgage, request an amortization schedule from your lender. That schedule will show each payment's principal/interest split along with a running total of the loan balance. It should help you calculate how much you can save through prepayments.

There are, however, a few things you should consider before starting a prepayment program. First, all consumer debt—with its higher interest and smaller totals—should be paid off first. After you clear your debts, you'll have what you used to spend on minimum credit payments to put toward the mortgage principal. Second, you should maximize any company-matched funds available through your employer's savings and investment plan. If you can increase your contribution level to the maximum, do so before making prepayments on your home. Matching-funds plans change from year to year, so take advantage of them whenever you can for as long as you can.

Finally, don't put any of your six-month emergency cash reserve (see the earlier discussion on savings) into home equity. Many people reason, "When I put money into my house, it is still my money and still available to me." It is— but it is not a liquid source of funds as is the savings account, and may be difficult to appropriate in an emergency. You need those six months of reserves in the bank.

Sometime after you settle into a comfortable payment pattern, you are sure to receive a refinancing offer. To decide if rewriting your loan balance into a new mortgage makes sense, divide the cost of refinancing by the amount you would save in monthly payments to find your break-even number. If the new mortgage payment would be $120 less per month than your current payment and the refinancing cost would be $2,400, divide $2,400 by $120 to get 20. Therefore, you would break even financially after twenty months of making refinanced mortgage payments. If you plan to remain in your current house for two years or more, this refinancing option does make sense; if you expect to move in eighteen months, you will lose money on the option.

Hence, when refinancing, always find an offer that fits your situation. If you come across a good offer that makes sense, do show it to your current mortgage company before finalizing the new deal. Your own mortgage company may be able to meet or beat the new offer, especially if you consider surveys, inspections, and closing costs.

If you do refinance, make sure it shortens, or at least retains, the life span of your current loan. If you originally financed your existing home for thirty years and have been living there ten years, do not refinance it for more than twenty years.

And after refinancing your loan, don't reduce the monthly payments you were making before. With the $120-less-payment scenario above, if you continue paying that extra $120 each month, you will pay off your house even faster.

One last financial aspect of home ownership is dealing with home-equity loans and lines. Such home-equity products are excellent ways to raise money for home improvements, and can also be applied to educational or job-training programs or used to meet medical emergencies. Be very careful, however. If you assume a loan or a second mortgage by using your home equity as collateral, and you ever default on payments, the lenders can evict you and sell your house. And never use a home-equity product to finance a consolidation loan. Some people, often lured by tax-deductible interest, roll all their credit-card debt into home-equity products. If these people continue their careless spending habits, though—as so often happens with consolidation loans—they are setting themselves up to eventually lose their homes.

Transportation

Your car is the other major item in the spending category. Private transportation is a requirement for most of today's society. Your challenge is to select the most economical option to satisfy this need. There are some fundamental points everyone should consider when choosing a vehicle.

The first decision is whether to buy or lease the vehicle. I strongly recommend purchasing. When you buy, you build equity against the day you own the vehicle outright. Leasing—when you have any ongoing need for transportation—can trap you in a vicious cycle that may prove very difficult to break.

The best reason I know for not leasing a vehicle is that such a long-term rental agreement lacks reciprocity. Most people lease vehicles for two or three years and make monthly payments based on estimated resale value. If you officially estimate driving a thousand miles a month over the life of a thirty-six month lease agreement—for a total of thirty-six thousand miles—and you drive forty-six thousand miles instead, an excess-mileage penalty will be due when you turn in the car on the grounds that the extra ten thousand miles reduce the vehicle's anticipated resale value. However, if you drive only twenty-six thousand miles in those three years, thus saving ten thousand miles' worth of value for the dealer, you receive no money back. Hence, your expense per mile driven escalates when you fail to attain the mileage limit.

If it were possible to estimate accurately how many miles you would drive during the leasing period, the difference might be negligible. I, for one, though, cannot even be sure how many miles I will drive in the next three days. Unless you have a well-proven, accurate process for determining the number of miles you will drive during the leasing period—and unless you get through the period with no unexpected emergencies or lifestyle changes—you are likely to come out behind.

I remember a former student who had leased a vehicle based on her estimated distance for commuting to work. Only a few months after leasing that car, she lost her job. Fortunately, she soon found an even better position, which provided a company car. Unfortunately—though the leased vehicle had been used for only a few months and was now no longer required—the dealer refused to take it back, but insisted on the terms of the lease agreement. When my student finally returned the car, at the end of the official thirty-six months, she had driven less than twelve thousand miles—far below the official total for which she had paid. "I had signed an agreement," she said, "and I was locked in."

Another student, who also leased a vehicle based on estimated commuting mileage, lived only a few miles from her job. Over time, however, she became frustrated with her work. When she finally found a job that better fit her skills, it required a fifty-mile daily commute, invalidating the calculations she had used for the lease and guaranteeing a hefty excess-mileage fee when the car was returned.

Is there any potential benefit to leasing a vehicle? When I pose that question to a class, the answer—if anyone has one—is always, "If I lease a car every three years, I can easily get a new vehicle when my lease runs out." Even taking that into account, however, the potential benefit nearly always costs more than it is worth. If you sign a three-year lease, with a $300 monthly payment, you will pay $10,800 ($300 x 36 months) by the end of the lease—assuming you incur no additional fees. If you need new transportation at the end of those thirty-six months, and you lease another vehicle for the next three years—say at $400 a month this time—it will cost you a minimum of $14,400 ($400 x 36 months) during that period. By the end of the second lease, you will have spent more than $25,000 in lease payments over a six-year period—and will have nothing to show for it except the need for yet another car.

By comparison, if you purchase a $20,000 vehicle and finance it for five years (which is a higher cost and longer period than most economically minded people require—in fact, you can buy a car without financing it at all; more on this shortly) at a 4.5 percent interest rate, the total amount you pay will be comparable to the six-year lease—and you will now own outright a car that, if maintained well, may serve you for another five to ten years.

Once you make the decision to purchase rather than lease a car, a slightly used vehicle—two or three years old—is the best investment. A brand-new car begins to depreciate (lose value) the minute you sign the purchase papers. If you doubt that, try negotiating the best possible deal on a new car, signing all the papers—and then immediately offering to sell the vehicle back to the dealer for the same price. I guarantee he or she will insist on paying less.

But whatever car you choose and price you pay, stick to the cash-only policy you use for smaller purchases. Sound impossible? Not with the following six-step process:

    1. Never trade in a car until any existing vehicle loan is paid off—even if you see another car you like better than what you're driving.

2. If you have been making monthly payments on a car, don't start spending that money on other things after the car is paid off. Continue to live on your old budget, and start to put the money into a savings account—an account set aside for the purchase of your next car.

3. Do everything you can to keep your current car running well. Keep the tires rotated, the oil changed, and all other preventive maintenance up to date.

4. Drive your existing car as long as you can. Replace worn-out parts, not the whole vehicle. Keep a car until the motor or framework is completely worn out.

5. When your car is so thoroughly used that the cost of maintenance outweighs the cost of replacement, take the funds you have been saving since your old car was paid off, to buy a good used car. If, for whatever reason, your old car reaches the hopeless stage before you have enough money for a decent replacement, apply what you can get in trade-in value (and insurance, if the old car was wrecked or stolen) toward the down payment, and finance the balance for the shortest time possible. As with a mortgage, pay the balance off early if you can.

6. Repeat the process. Once you master it, you will be able to pay cash for cars as long as you can drive.

CHAPTER EIGHT

Setting Goals

＋═══╤═══╤

Now that you know the basic principles of Christian money management, the next step is putting them into practice. First, make a budget for the next three months, allocating a set percentage of income to each of the five major categories. Then, add at least one "specific action" item to each category—steps you can take to stay within budget. This table comprises your goals for the next three months. At the end of that period, review your success and progress, establish new objectives, and adjust goals as necessary. (You may want to make tables for six-month and twelve-month goals as well.) This written plan will give you a sense of reassurance and will help you work toward your goals.

My financial classes use a "numbers game" to help students realize the value of planning. I start by distributing a piece of paper to each student, and telling everyone to keep theirs face down until I say "go." When they turn the papers over, I tell them, they will find the numbers from one to one hundred scattered over the page. The object of the game is starting with the number one and circling, in sequence, as many numbers as possible in one minute.

Few students who play this game get higher than the

number twenty. When asked how they felt during the exercise, they usually say they felt stressed, nervous, and directionless.

I then explain that there's a trick to the game. If the participants fold their papers in half lengthwise and then crosswise, and then open the papers again, they will find that the number one appears in the upper-left quadrant. The number two will appear in the upper right, the number three in the lower left, the number four in the lower right, the number five in the upper left, and so on. Once the students understand this, I ask if they think they can finish the game faster next time. They invariably are confident that they can.

After distributing the second set of numbered papers, however, I tell students they have only forty-five seconds— three-quarters as much time—for this round. Despite this, they nearly always get further numerically than on the first try, when they had more time but no plan.

Then I ask who currently uses a financial plan to guide his or her life. Almost never do I receive a positive response from anyone.

I explain that the "numbers game" exercise is like most people's experience with money. Most individuals receive very few instructions before they start managing their own funds. As a result, they feel nervous, directionless, and unsure of themselves. Many people never proceed beyond that stage in handling their money.

If, however, you implement a set plan for managing funds, based on the principles in this book, you will quickly reduce your stress, achieve a higher level of confidence, and learn to get further with your money in less time. You may not win total victory overnight but, as the principles become habits, you will grow more and more comfortable with them.

One warning—avoid the pitfall of overcorrection. Most people easily identify the cash flow areas that need to be addressed, but then feel guilty when they are unable to correct the related problems in a day. Remember, bad habits are not developed overnight and cannot be conquered overnight. Major adjustments are more effective when made during a period of time.

Beware also of the love of money—the longing to constantly pursue money and the things it can buy. Simply ignoring the desire will not work forever unless you can rid yourself of the mentality described in 1 Timothy 6:10: "For the love of money is a root of all kinds of evil. Some people, eager for money, have wandered from the faith and pierced themselves with many griefs." To keep greed from gaining—or regaining—control of your life, stay focused on the principles discussed early in this book:

1) Pray before you purchase.
2) Spend only what you have.
3) Record your spending.
4) Read Scripture daily.
5) Select an accountability partner.

Finally, remember that God owns everything, including "your" finances. Only with His help can you master them!

POSTSCRIPT

Understanding Your
Credit Report

+≍+

In conclusion, let's examine credit reports, which records your payment history on all purchases and debts combined. Most lenders regularly report their customers' payment histories—good and bad—to a credit bureau, which serves as a clearinghouse for all consumer credit material that is received. A credit bureau does not rate your credit, but potential creditors can access reports to determine if you are a good risk.

You yourself can—and should—access your own credit report on a regular basis. Thanks to the Fair and Accurate Credit Transaction Act, which was passed in response to growing concern about identity theft and inaccurate reports, you can now receive your report free of charge. And because not only lenders and insurance companies, but potential employers, are now checking credit reports regularly, it makes sense to correct errors before finding out the hard way that you have black marks on your credit record. It's a good idea to obtain a copy of your credit report each year, preferably on an easy-to-remember date, such as a birthday, anniversary, or holiday.

There are three major credit bureaus—Equifax, Experian, and TransUnion—which collect information and issue reports. Because not all creditors report to the same agency, it pays to acquire a separate report from each bureau. Fortunately, you don't have to contact each one separately; all three bureaus share one central dispatch, where free reports can be obtained. Log on to www.annualcreditreport.com (which also provides immediate online access to reports), or call 1-877-322-8228 (after which a report should be mailed within fifteen days of your request).

Once you have received your reports, review them for accuracy. If you find any incorrect information, dispute it *in writing*. Clear instructions and the correct form will be included in your report. By law, the credit bureau must investigate all disputed charges.

You can also check your credit score, although this requires a nominal fee. Credit scores are calculated by mathematically evaluating the information contained in a credit report, comparing the data with thousands of past credit reports, and issuing a "FICO score" to indicate future level of risk in issuing credit to a subject. The term "FICO" comes from Fair Isaac Corporation software, which is used to calculate most credit scores in the United States.

The higher a FICO score, the lower the risk and, therefore, the greater the likelihood of loan approval. Each lender, however, uses an individual rating strategy relative to the level of risk that the lender finds acceptable for a given credit product.

A FICO score rates consumers in five categories. The table below lists these categories in their approximate order of importance.

Category	Lenders' Question	Approximate Percentage of Importance
Payment History	What is this person's track record?	35%
Amounts Owed	How much is too much?	30%
Length of Credit History	How established is this person's credit?	15%
New Credit	Is this person in the process of assuming more debt?	10%
Types of Credit	Does this person use a healthy mix of credit types?	10%

The credit-score range is from 300 to 850, and the average consumer's score is about 675.

If you think your score needs improvement, following are a few tips for raising it:

- Pay your bills promptly. There is no substitute for consistent and timely payment.
- If you have been delinquent with any of your payments, contact each creditor to negotiate a solution. Would *you* loan money to anyone who was already delinquent in his or her payments to others?
- Pay off your debt rather than distributing it around. Owing the same amount of money to fewer people may lower your score.
- Maintain the lowest possible balance in each account. High outstanding debt has a major impact on your score.
- Use existing credit only if absolutely necessary. Opening new credit can only hurt your score.

Remember, when your credit report changes, so does your score. Don't expect dramatic results right away, though. In any given three-month time period, only about one in four people experiences a 20-point or higher improvement in credit score. While late payments, charge-offs, and bankruptcy can lower your score quickly, improving your score takes time. That is why it is a good idea to start now.

Don't, however, believe "credit repair clinics" that claim they can "legally" remove bad credit. First of all, there's a difference between bad credit and incorrect information. You can usually get rid of incorrect information by following the report's guidelines for disputing errors—without paying anyone else to do it. "Bad credit," which results from handling credit poorly, cannot be removed if it is based on factual information. Credit information, good or bad, stays on your report for seven years; bankruptcy information stays on your report for ten years; and there is no way to erase the past. So, don't pay anyone to "fix your credit." Most "credit repair clinics" charge you large fees to obtain credit reports and then send letters to dispute any errors or questionable information—something any consumer can do for the cost of a few postage stamps. And if you are in a bad credit position with only yourself to blame, your sole option is beginning to rebuild your reputation from the ground up.

Returning to the impact a credit score has on your financial situation: There is an inverse correlation between your interest rate and your credit score. The lower (i.e., worse) your credit score, the higher the interest rate you will be charged on new loans. Because a low credit score indicates past difficulties managing your credit, the lender views you as a high-risk investment and—to cover the risk of losing money on the loan—offers you a higher interest rate. Suppose you are financing a thirty-year, $125,000 mortgage with a fixed rate, and your credit score is between 720 and 850. You will probably be eligible for an interest rate of 5.488 percent, which means a monthly mortgage payment of $624.00. If your credit score were between 700 and 719, however, you would be eligible for a 5.613 percent interest rate and a monthly mortgage payment of $632.00. Over the life of the mortgage, the higher (5.613 percent) interest rate would cost you an additional $2,880.00. The difference increases as your credit score decreases. If your score were between 500 and 559, your rate would be just over 9 percent, your monthly mortgage slightly more than $900, and you would pay an additional $102,000 over the life of the loan.

Scenario	Score	Rate	Monthly Mortgage	30-Year Difference from (Best-Case) Scenario A
A	720-850	5.488%	$624.00	$0.00
B	700-719	5.613%	$632.00	$2,880.00
C	675-699	6.151%	$670.00	$16,560.00
D	620-674	7.301%	$754.00	$46,800.00
E	560-619	8.531%	$848.00	$80,640.00
F	500-559	9.289%	$908.00	$102,240.00

Perhaps it seems backward that the borrowers with the worst credit should pay the highest monthly bills. But, if it were your money, wouldn't you charge those most likely to default on a loan a higher interest rate to cover your risk by collecting as much as you could as soon as you could?

Appendix

(1) David Olson's 2003 National Survey of Marital Strengths
(2) Business News, November 24, 2003, by Alan Lavine and Gail Liberman

Printed in the United States
58297LVS00002B/1-51